Grassroots Marketing For The Restaurant Industry

Grassroots Marketing For The Restaurant Industry

Adam Barringer

Writers Club Press
San Jose New York Lincoln Shanghai

Grassroots Marketing For The Restaurant Industry

Writers Club Press
an imprint of iUniverse, Inc.

For information address:
iUniverse, Inc.
5220 S. 16th St., Suite 200
Lincoln, NE 68512
www.iuniverse.com

Cover Design by Tommy Robertson

ISBN: 0-595-22318-4

Printed in the United States of America

CONTENTS

CHAPTER 1

Grassroots Marketing

> "There is only one boss. The customer. And he can fire everybody in the company, from the chairman on down, simply by spending his money somewhere else."
>
> —Sam Walton

I know as a restaurant operator, your time is valuable, therefore I will get to the "meat and potatoes" of this book. Traditional marketing is based on the principles of the Four P's: Product, Price, Place (distribution) and Promotion. In today's dynamic business environment, marketing consists of customer, content, communication and cost. The two concepts are similar, however, today, the customer must be at the center of your restaurant and viewed as part of your team because they are the major contributors to the bottom line. Without customers, there is no restaurant! Grassroots marketing is part of the promotional or communication mix within the overall marketing plan. Promotion is the most visible part of the marketing plan and often confused for the entire plan. Developing the promotional mix should be the last step of the plan.

You communicate to your target market about your restaurant through the elements of promotion that you choose. So what is grassroots marketing?

Grassroots-*"People or society at a local level."*

Marketing-*1.)"The act or business of promoting sales of a product, as by Advertising or packaging." 2.) Anything you do to make your customers aware of your product and to purchase your product on a repeat basis.*

Grassroots Marketing—*"Promoting your business within your community using cost effective strategies."*

Through trial and error as a restaurant manager coupled with the research I conducted while obtaining my MBA, I have come to the realization that *there is no single marketing strategy that will achieve the desired results*. Mark Rosenthal, a successful restaurateur in Nashville, TN, stated "it may take four or five or ten different approaches to attract customers to your restaurant. It is the synergy created by multiple marketing activities performed on a consistent basis that will achieve the intended goal." This is because no two people are alike. Each of us has a different personality and we are motivated by different stimuli in the environment.

Marketing is not easy. If it were easy, a high school student working part time would be able to do the job. If it were easy, your competition would be doing it. Most grassroots marketing concepts are simple however, it is necessary to *develop a plan and commit to the plan*. I recommend designing a simple marketing calendar to plan and budget the activities you want to get involved with. I have included a sample plan at the end of this chapter as well as a blank plan for you to use. This information should be kept and reviewed on a regular basis. It will help determine which activities worked best and provide a foundation for the following months and the upcoming years.

As the leader in your restaurant, you must get your entire staff to commit to the marketing plan. 100% effort is required to be successful in today's competitive environment. You must create the marketing culture in your restaurant. A culture shared by all your employees produces a sense of purpose and a drive to achieve the goals you set, which will lead to a more successful restaurant.

A word of caution, before you begin marketing your restaurant, you better make sure you are prepared to handle the business. There is nothing worse than effectively marketing your restaurant only to have your customer's expectations go unmet. There is an old saying that states "great marketing can ruin a poorly managed business."

The following are the different types of "traditional" promotional elements that businesses currently use:

Advertising-This is the part of the promotional mix people typically think of when considering a marketing plan. It includes all openly sponsored, paid forms of communication about your restaurant. There are advantages and disadvantages to each type of advertising. The major disadvantage is that each of these cost money. I recommend developing relationships with these media companies & their reps and work a "trade-out" with them.

Newspapers
Radio
Television & local cable
Magazines
Transit (cabs, buses, bus stops)
Billboards
Display signs
Posters & leaflets
Directories (hotel, airports, rental car agencies)
Brochures & booklets
Packaging inserts

Sales Promotions (Incentives)-Through this element of the promotions mix, you are rewarding the customer for choosing your restaurant, encouraging customers to try a new product, and to increase your name and recognition in the target market. It is also a way for you to entice your staff to help increase sales.

Staff Contests
Samplings
Demonstrations
Tie-ins
Gift Certificates
Rewards
Recognition
Coupons

Publicity-This element of the promotional mix includes any media coverage your restaurant receives for free. Public Relations are the strategy for presenting the restaurant to the public. Publicity is considered valuable because it is an implied endorsement from the media and it is free!

> Press kits
> Charitable donations
> Sponsorships
> Community relations
> Events

Sales Force (Personal Selling)-This includes any sales that comes from your staff. This category is considered to be the most expensive promotional tool. In restaurants, if you want to be successful, you must selectively recruit then train your staff well. They are your personal sales force.

> Sales presentations
> Telephone Contacts
> Special events
> Incentive programs
> Point-of-purchase displays (Table tents, posters)
> (Sales training)

Direct Mail-Any promotional message relayed in the form of mail. Direct mailings target a specific audience and have the highest response rate.

Mailings
Newsletters
Postcards
Email
Fax transmissions
Flyers

Visual Promotions & Affinity Merchandise-This is an element that many restaurants fail to recognize as part of the promotional mix. However, it is a very important element that needs to be addressed. These items are good for grabbing the customer's attention and an inexpensive way to promote the restaurant.

Signs
Business Cards
Stationary
Name tags
Packaging
Paper goods
Hats, T-shirts
Pens
Matches

Grassroots marketing encompasses all elements of the promotional mix and is implemented using "guerrilla tactics". **Guerrilla marketing** is a way for entrepreneurs with limited resources to reach their customers and build relationships as effectively as large corporations with significant resources. However, grassroots marketing takes place in your community. The following grassroots marketing tactics and promotions are discussed in future chapters are:

- Internal Marketing
    - Proper maintenance of your facility
    - Creating a "high" in your restaurant by properly managing your staff
    - Marketing to your vendors and you supply chain
    - Gift Certificates

- External Marketing
    - Athletic Sponsorships
    - Charity Events
    - Community Involvement

- Technology and how it is being used for marketing.
- Direct Mail

The success of a grassroots-marketing plan will depend on your ability to design and implement a strategy that will cause your targeted audience to choose your restaurant! Grassroots marketing is a way for your restaurant to compete in your community with larger restaurant companies who have a seemingly unlimited marketing budget.

Summary Points

- There is no single approach to achieve the desired results
- Marketing is not easy
- Develop a promotional plan
- Create the culture within your restaurant
- Commit to the plan
- Prepare for increased business

Exhibit A, Sample Marketing Plan

Date	Promotional Activity	Charitable Organization	Number of People	Cost	Target Market
1/25	Silent Auction (donate dinner for two)	Cystic Fibrosis	350	$100	Mid-Upper income families
4/1	FRA Golf Tournament (provide box lunch to golfers)	Florida Restaurant Assoc.	300	$500	Local business owners & executives
6/20	Taste of Tampa Bay	Boys & Girls Club	2500	$800	Mid-Upper income adults 30-55, local restaurants & businesses
9/12	Monday Night Football (Two for One appetizer special, $1.00 per appetizer sold is donated to Charity)	Cystic Fibrosis	2000	$1,000	Cystic Fibrosis mailing list, current customers
	Sponsorship	Organization	Number of People	Cost	Target Market
2/1	Youth soccer Team	City of Tampa	250	$200	Middle income families
8/11	Teacher of the Month	Tampa High School	3000	$1,000	Teachers, Age 25-55
	Advertising	Company		Cost	Target Market
1/15	Annual Yellow Page Ad	Superpages.com		$500	Entire city
2/8	Radio (Valentines Ad)	1010 Sports Radio		$2,200	Men 25-45

10/7	Billboard (Holiday Gift Certificate. Run for 3 months)	Lamar Outdoor		$6,000	30,00 People per day, North Tampa
Dues		**Company**		**Cost**	**Target Market**
3/30	Annual Chamber of Commerce	Tampa Chamber of Commerce		$500	Local Businesses
11/25	NRA Dues	National Restaurant Association		$1,500	Not applicable

Total Promotional Budget		$14,300

Exhibit B, Blank Sample Marketing Plan

Date	Promotional Activity	Charitable Organization	Number of People	Cost	Target Market
	Sponsorship	Organization	Number of People	Cost	Target Market
	Advertising	Company		Cost	Target Market
	Dues	Company		Cost	Target Market

Total Promotional Budget		

CHAPTER 2

"Your Four Walls"

> "Markets change, tastes change, so the companies and the individuals who choose to compete in those markets must change."
> —Dr. An Wang

Before I discuss some external grassroots-marketing strategies, look around. What is the condition of your restaurant? Your customers, employees and vendors pass judgment on your restaurant by the messages you send them. Customers listed the following impressions according to importance:

- Restaurant pride
- Restaurant quality (service and food)
- Legitimate prices
- Financial stability
- Type of store manager
- Is it worth returning?
- Is it worth going in?
- Does it match the store advertising?

- Is it a store of the future?
- Is this restaurant concerned about my safety?
- Is it a national chain or an independent?

Your customers are constantly evaluating your restaurant, making judgments and decisions whether or not to dine. In a two-year study, over 60% of customers noted the restaurant's appearance as a deciding factor when choosing a restaurant. An article in Food Industry News stated that 80% of respondents to a survey said they would not want to return to a restaurant with dirty bathrooms. Several respondents believed that if the bathroom was a mess then the kitchen's cleanliness is questionable. (Only 20% of respondents said they would return to a restaurant with dirty bathrooms... I can only speculate that you may not want those 20% in your restaurant!)

Your restaurant needs to be kept fresh and current. A store with décor from 1992 will lose its appeal in 2002. The following was an article in The Nation's Restaurant News regarding renovations. I find this interesting due to the fact my career managing restaurants began at Bennigan's. In the early 1990's Bennigan's should have focused on updating décor and food quality. A decade later, they are chasing the competition.

The past year saw the emergence of reimaging plans by some of the segment's biggest combatants. Metromedia Restaurant Group's Bennigan's
concept is now in the midst of a chainwide face-lift, which features an
updated look and an increased focus on food. Some of the chain's
recently completed remodels are fetching an average 5-percent increase
in sales.

Bennigan's also finds itself in a considerable growth mode, planning to
add 61 new restaurants while updating 41 existing units in 2000. The
build-out compares with scant growth in fiscal 1999, during which the
chain added only 11 stores to its holdings.

Following along similar lines, Red Lobster is moving ahead with a
chainwide refurbishing program that features expanded bar areas and
new touches to both interior and exterior designs. The chain, operated
by Darden Restaurants, has completed 110 remodels in the past 18
months, spending around $300,000 per restaurant. The program fol-
lows along with the chain's new advertising campaign, which features
edgy spots designed to recast the aging Red Lobster as "The New Red."

-Nation's Restaurant News

Your customers are not the only people who notice the condition and
appearance of your restaurant, your employees and vendors also notice.
Poor working conditions have a negative affect on employee moral.

Not all of your employees serve, but all of your employees sell! All your
employees interact socially with their circle of influence, family, friends,
and community members outside of the work environment. As an owner
or manager, you want your employees saying great things about you and
your restaurant. You want them to take pride when discussing what they
do and where they work. This is a great form of publicity, and a piece of
the grassroots-marketing puzzle.

In addition, you want your employees to have enough pride to wear a T-
shirt or a hat with your restaurant's name and/or logo on it. In fact, you

should encourage your staff to endorse your restaurant on their way to work, on their way home or on their day off. Although this may seem like a simple marketing strategy, guess what? It is! **Affinity merchandise** is any type of merchandise with your restaurant's name or logo on it. When your employees, customers and vendors visibly display your restaurant's name or logo either on a hat, T-shirt, or gym bag this is a form of free endorsement!

Summary Points

- Keep your restaurant fresh and current
- All customers notice the appearance, 60% attribute this to choosing where to dine
- Poor working conditions affect employee moral
- All employees sell
- Affinity Merchandise is anything with your restaurant's name or logo on it.

CHAPTER 3

The Supply Chain

> Courage rather than analysis dictates the truly important rules for identifying priorities:
> -Pick the future as against the past;
> -Focus on opportunity rather than on problem;
> -Choose your own direction-rather than climb on the bandwagon; and
> -Aim high, aim for something that will make a difference, rather than for something that is 'safe' and easy to do."
> -Peter Drucker in The Effective Executive

There have been many books and articles written on supply chain management. The emergence of the information age has emphasized the importance of building and nurturing the value chain. The basic concept of supply chain and value chain management is the ability to create value along the supply chain, beginning with the distributor of raw materials all the way to the retail of the finished good. Grassroots marketing to your supply chain and value chain is a rather simple concept.

Lets start with the sales representatives that visit your restaurant. Whether you expect them or not, whether the product they are selling interests you or not, understand that they are in your restaurant and you have a chance to sell them! You have the opportunity to involve them in your grassroots marketing campaign. If they show up prior to or after business hours, what condition is the restaurant in? If they come to your "back door" what does that part of the restaurant look like? How clean is your "back dock"? How do you treat the sales reps? Do you offer them a drink? Perhaps you offer them something to eat. If the sales representative leaves with or without a sale, what will he say to others about your restaurant or how professionally he was treated?

The next group of people to focus on in the supply chain are the delivery drivers. Once again, when they make a delivery, what is the condition of the restaurant? If delivering to the "back door", what does that area look like? What is the condition of your "back dock"? Do you offer them a drink? Do you offer to cook something for them? How do you treat them when they are late? How are they treated when there is a "mispick" on your order or if an item is missing altogether? What will this group of people say to others when they leave your restaurant? What will they say to fellow workers, family and friends?

As the owner or manager, in today's competitive marketplace, you have the opportunity to maintain a clean and organized restaurant. It should not matter who comes into your front or back door; these areas should be clean, organized and well maintained. You want your "supply chain partners" telling everyone they talk to, how clean,organized and well managed your restaurant is.

You also have the opportunity to treat your supply chain partners better than any other account they call on. If a sales representative is making a sales call at your restaurant, be polite even if you do not intend on purchasing anything. Be polite even if you do not intend on buying anything. Offer them a drink. Your hospitality towards the sales reps will have a positive impact on the business relationship. You can use this relationship to build a partnership with these sales reps and their companies. You will be able to ask them to partner in sponsoring charity events, donate prizes for sales contests and assist in sales training activities for your service staff. Your goal with these supply chain members should be one of partnership, to make these suppliers advocates of your restaurant.

Always offer the delivery drivers a drink and if time permits, offer them some food. By doing so, they will strive to make sure your deliveries are on time with no mistakes. They will tell their fellow coworkers and their family and friends how well you treat them. Once you have won the drivers with your generosity, they too will become advocates of your restaurant. If you feel they represent your target market, then give them a hat or a T-shirt with the company name and logo.

When placing orders over the phone, get to know the person who takes your order. Find out how many employees are in the office. Get to know the office manager. Make them part of your supply chain partners. Treat them better than any other account treats them. Occasionally, send food (breakfast, lunch or dinner depending on your specialty and geographic location), or cater their office party. Sending greeting cards during the holidays is also a nice gesture. Consider sending a card for a holiday such a St. Patrick's Day or the 4th of July. Cards sent during the holiday season are sometimes expected and the intended message may be lost in the onslaught of other cards!

You may even consider rewarding you vendors on a monthly basis. For example, a vendor of the month program. Each month you can select a vendor of the month and display a plaque in you restaurant with the company and the company's representative engraved on it. You could even give the winning vendor partner a complimentary meal for two along with some affinity merchandise!

As the owner or manager, you have the opportunity to make your supply chain part of your grassroots marketing efforts! There are added benefits to treating each member of your supply chain as partners. They will be more responsive to any problems that may arise during the business relationship and supportive of your community service and charitable contribution efforts. Remember that you are their retail outlet for product.

SUMMARY POINTS

- Keep your restaurant clean, organized and well maintained from the back dock to the front door. This is the sales reps and delivery drivers' first and last impression of your restaurant.
- Always offer drinks and food to your sales reps and delivery drivers.
- Get to know the people who take your phone orders. If it is a local company, make them your supply chain partner.
- Your efforts will be rewarded beyond the marketing function.

CHAPTER 4

"Inside Your Four Walls"

Anonymous marketing just doesn't work anymore. Consumers want to know not only what they are buying, but also whom they're buying it from. The people, not the logo. Consumer relation's development is as important as the product itself.

-Frank Purdue

"The Owner"

As an owner/operator when you get directly involved with a customer, there is an 83% chance for repeat business. Surveys reveal that customers feel there is no greater honor than being acknowledged by the owner. Three things happen that cannot be matched by anyone else. First, the customers have their psychological "need to belong" satisfied. Abraham Maslow developed a hierarchy of needs. Once the physiological needs (food, shelter and sex) and safety needs are satisfied, the need to belong is the next need that people strive to satisfy. This is one of the most powerful influences in your customer's decision making process. Recognition by the owner makes customers feel important. It makes them feel like they belong. Second, if the owner does something special for the customer, whether it is remembering a name, buying a round of drinks, "comping" an appetizer or dessert, it reflects the caring attitude of the restaurant. The third thing you can do as an owner/operator like nobody else is say thank you! Gratitude expressed by the owner conveys the business was appreciated. This type of customer service will lead to repeat business.

As an owner or manager you should be aware that everyone has a psychological need to belong. Therefore it is important to know your customers. How many customers do you know by name? What do you know about them? Where they work? How about their families, where are they from? What are their favorite sports teams? Customer loyalty takes a long time to build. It does not happen overnight. This type of marketing in known as **relationship marketing, or one-to-one marketing**. Building relationships with your customers, one person at a time.

"The Lifelong Customer"

It is imperative that you understand the concept of the "lifelong customer." I first read about this concept "the value of a life long customer" in an article published by the Harvard Business Review. Since that first article, I have read dozens of article and books regarding this concept. In essence, you need to treat every sales transaction as the beginning or the continuation of a lifelong relationship. You should not focus on a one-time sale. A lifelong customer will tell his family, friends, coworkers and community members about your relationship. Think about this, a stockbroker will spend the first several years building business relationships with clients. After building these relationships, (as long as he treats his customers with care,) he can reduce his "cold calling" efforts, because many of his new sales will result from referrals and repeat business from highly satisfied customers.

After 3 years, an estimated 80% of business comes from his existing customer base. If the stockbroker fails to cultivate the lifelong relationships, he will have to cold call forever. Trust me, this is not how a stockbroker wants to spend an entire career. The initial sale is just the beginning. Once you have earned a customer's loyalty and trust, your customer base will expand and your business will thrive. Let us not forget we are in the business of sales! According to Kotler on Marketing, the stages of creating a lifelong customer are:

First-time customer-The probability that the new customer will buy again is strongly related to his level of satisfaction with the first purchase.

Repeat customer-Retained customers buy more over time if they are highly satisfied. This happens through cross selling (different menu items) and up selling. The cost of serving a retained customer decreases over time, they recommend the restaurant to others and they become less sensitive to price increases.

Client-In the restaurant business, we use the term customer or guest. Professional firms use the word "client". What is the difference? Professional firms know more about their clients. Second, they devote more time to helping and satisfying clients. Third, their relation to the client is more continuous and leads to more familiarity and empathy. Perhaps it is just a play on words, but how many of your customers would you consider to be clients?

Advocate-The more a client likes the restaurant, the more likely he is to talk favorably about it, either when asked for an opinion or without. The aim of every restaurant should be to create fans! Fan is short for fanatic, which for example is how Harley-Davidson motorcycle owners feel about the Harley-Davidson Company and its products.

Member-To further "loyalize" clients, restaurants might launch a membership program that has privileges.

The cost to obtain a new customer is 5 to 10 times more than to maintain an existing customer. Knowing this, how important is addressing complaints? If someone leaves your restaurant unhappy, research has proven that they will tell at least nine people. And those nine people will tell several more and so on. Complaints should be viewed as an opportunity for improvement, not something that should be ignored. **Complaint marketing** is an opportunity to speak with your customers and continually improve. Pizza Hut for example, has an 800 number for customers to call when they have a complaint. The customer service rep will listen to the complaint and forward it to the appropriate store. The manager is then required to contact the customer and resolve the issue within 48 hours.

Employees

Your service staff is your sales force. 70% of your customers view the service staff as the store. The following are traits customers prefer in a waiter or waitress:

- Greets with a smile
- Makes the customer feel at ease
- Exhibits professionalism
- Can answer questions and is knowledgeable about the product
- Knows store policies & procedures
- Qualifies the customer for the sale
- Makes them feel appreciated after the sale

As I stated in chapter two, employee moral is directly related to working conditions. While this includes the physical condition of your restaurant, it definitely includes how they are treated! If a manager yells at an employee, how many customers will be affected? The days when managers utilized only "hard people" skills in their style of management are obsolete, which is why I am writing a book! Treat employees how they want to be treated, provide a pleasant working environment, exhibit pride in the restaurant and your employees will mirror that attitude when interacting with the customers. Your employee's positive attitude will have a positive affect on repeat sales.

I have included a survey regarding how customers measure service in order of priority:

1. The employee shows he or she wants to be at work
2. The employee is available to offer genuine suggestions
3. The restaurant is clean
4. The menu is easy to read
5. The employee is knowledgeable and also knows the restaurant's policy and procedures
6. The customer feels the restaurant is trying to please them
7. The employees are well dressed
8. The restaurant is comfortable

I cannot stress the importance of providing your employees a great working environment. It will lead to an increase in profits due to cost reduction typically associated with recruiting, hiring & training. A tenured staff can and will get to know your customers, what they order, and any special instructions, which will make your customers feel welcome and comfortable. This goes along with satisfying the need to belong.

Summary Points

- Get directly involved with your customers
- Practice one-to-one marketing to create lifelong customers
- Provide your employees with a work environment they take pride in!

Owner Profile

Keith and Ginger Dunn are the franchise owners of The Melting Pot Restaurant in Myrtle Beach, SC. Their humble beginnings as restaurant owners have defined how incredible these two individuals are, which has lead to the many successes they are now enjoying.

Keith & Ginger believed in The Melting Pot concept and like many entrepreneurs, they opened the restaurant using all their savings including Keith's 401K. For the first three months, they were unable to hire a dishwasher not to mention they probably couldn't afford one! Ginger's response to Keith was, "I will wash dishes because it is important for you to meet and talk to all the customers." Ginger washed dishes for the first three months without a day off! Keith ran the restaurant and built relationships with many of his customers and all of his employees.

Keith & Ginger now own a second Melting Pot, located in Columbus, Ohio and have plans for expansion. Both of the restaurants are experiencing double digit growth in spite of the economy and terrorist attacks. Keith & Ginger have been nominated for numerous achievement awards and accolades from the company and their community. Keith is proud to say that Ginger no longer washes dishes at the restaurant but she often bakes cookies and brings gifts to the employees, especially the dishwashers.

On my last visit to their restaurant, I was impressed as I watched Keith, his two managers and service staff recognize and address nearly every customer by name. Later that night, I asked Keith what has been his most successful grassroots marketing effort. He said "taking care of my employees. Anytime I lose an employee, I have to ask myself where did I fall short?"

CHAPTER 5

Community Involvement

> "Without a sense of caring, there can be no sense of community."
> -Anthony D D'Angelo

The previous chapters briefly discussed several forms of internal grassroots marketing. We discussed how you can impact sales through your attention to your physical plant, how you manage your staff, and how you and your staff interact with customers. Marketing strategies and tactics will succeed or fail based on how well your restaurant is managed. Now I will introduce you to several types of external grassroots "concepts" that are effective. *Regardless of the type of restaurant your are managing, you are part of a community.* If you want to build sales and profits, get involved with the community. People do business with people they know; other business owners will do business with business owners they know. Networking in the community is essential for all types of professionals and business owners. I used the example of the stockbroker in an earlier chapter. However, it does not matter if it is a stockbroker, an insurance salesperson or a real estate agent, they all network at community meetings.

Chamber of Commerce

Marketing is not easy and it takes time away from the restaurant. You have to be committed to growing your business. The first place I recommend getting involved with is The Chamber of Commerce. Your local chamber of commerce exists to assist in the growth of your restaurant. It has been my experience that the chamber offers a wealth of information about your community. It is a great resource for ideas, referrals, and potential customers. The chamber hosts many events each month. Some examples include business card exchanges, membership drive meetings, business after hour receptions, committee meetings, luncheons and an assortment of other community related events. As a restaurant manager or owner, you can participate in a number of ways. You can simply attend these functions and network as most of the members; you can provide food and beverages as a cosponsor; or you can host an event at your restaurant. Newsletters and invitations are sent out each month informing members of upcoming activities.

As an owner, I found success in cosponsoring "Business-After-Hours" receptions. My restaurant would provide the food and service staff; the cosponsor (Gold's Gym and Cannon Buick Car Dealership each located in Lakeland, FL) would provide the facility, the beverages and the entertainment. I cosponsored two events like this each year. We eventually earned the reputation as the chamber events that all members attended! As an added bonus, after the event, a large majority went back to the restaurant to have a full dinner!

Mailing lists are available to all chamber members usually at a cost of about $.10 per label. You can also elect to purchase computer disks, which contain the information for you to print out your own mailing labels. Direct mailings to local business are a great way build sales. You can communicate to these potential customers everything from special events, promotions, wine tastings, new menu items to holiday gift certificates. Essentially, the chamber of commerce mailing list is a database of all the businesses in your community. Creating databases of customers is big business in today's information age. Database management has become an industry within the technological sector. As we continue into the information age, database management is a service you may want to consider outsourcing.

National Restaurant Association & State Restaurant Association

The National Restaurant Association is a great source of information pertaining to the restaurant industry. You can get more information on The National Restaurant Association through their Web site at www.nationalrestaurantassociation.com. Your state restaurant association probably has a local chapter in your community. If they do not, start one! They usually meet once a month. Involvement in the restaurant association requires time and effort. As I stated in the beginning of the book, marketing is not easy! The restaurant association meetings are fun and informative. They discuss industry-related topics, offer networking opportunities, allow access to industry statistics, and provide training and workforce development. The restaurant association also has strong ties to the community. They sponsor school-to-work programs, community golf tournaments, scholarships and mentoring, and they are involved in local political campaigns. In addition to the regular meetings, there are subcommittees that welcome participation. These subcommittees may include membership, fundraising, leads groups, and politics. There are opportunities to become the chairperson for these committees, for your restaurant to host the meetings or just to participate. This gives your restaurant exposure through networking with your industry peers, vendors and suppliers.

Clubs, Organizations and Associations

There are many clubs, organizations and associations that meet on a weekly or monthly basis in your community. Hosting different group meetings is a great way to meet people and market your business. The newspaper is a viable resource to find a listing of the groups and associations in you community. You can provide the group or organization an area of the restaurant where they can conduct their meeting. In addition, you could provide them with drinks and appetizers. Having people actually taste your food is better advertisement then words or pictures. Upon the conclusion of the meetings, these clubs and organizations may invite their family or friends to meet them for lunch or dinner. Organizations and associations that you network with may very well represent other networks. Take the Realtors Association for example. They represent real estate agents in your community. And real estate agents network with homeowners moving into and out of the neighborhood. Some other examples of clubs, organizations and associations are:

- Democratic Club
- Republican Club
- Toastmasters
- Rotary Club
- Kiwanis Club
- Realtors Association
- Builders Association
- Civic Organizations
- Church groups

- Performing Arts Foundation
- Business Associations
- Auxiliary Groups
- Junior Leagues
- Builders Associations
- Homeowners Associations
- Lions Club
- Sports Clubs

Hosting diners for pharmaceutical & medical sales representatives is another grassroots marketing function. The sales representatives will invite local doctors to your restaurant, either for diner or take out. While the food is being prepared, the sales reps have the opportunity to discuss their products with the doctors. You not only benefit with the revenues derived from the dinner you also have the chance to market your restaurant to the doctors in your community! You can bet that if the doctors enjoy their experience, they will tell their family, friends, patients and the employees they work with. The sales reps might even make a sale.

Summary Points

- Community involvement takes time
- The Chamber of Commerce is a great place to start
- Local restaurant associations offer valuable information about the industry and the community
- Host meetings for local clubs and organizations

CHAPTER 6

Charity Events

> "Goodwill is the only asset that the competition cannot undersell or destroy"
>
> —Marshall Field

Charity events are one of the best ways to utilize the grassroots marketing function. Sponsoring community events, charities and nonprofit organizations can build goodwill for your restaurant and broaden your customer base. Press releases tied to charity functions help to strengthen your image and reputation. However, your charitable time and resources will be wasted unless you gain exposure before, during, and after the event.

There are many charitable and non-profit organizations. Select one or two charities or non-profit organizations you want to work with. You may select one for personal reasons or because they have a large mailing list. In any event, stick with just a few, it will be easier to manage. I will caution about the use of your restaurant's gift certificates as donations. Every type of group, organization, charity and non-profit will solicit you for donations. This can become extremely frustrating. You should budget the amount of gift certificates you want to donate each month. Once you have reached you budget, you must learn to say no in a positive way!

Golf tournaments are an easy way to partner with a charity. Golf tournaments are a popular fund raising activity for charities. You can have very limited involvement, by donating gift certificates for prizes and raffles, provide some type of affinity merchandise or direct marketing material for the "goodie bags". You can go so far as to sponsor a "hole-in-one", "closest to the pin" or longest drive contest. If you want to be more involved and gain increased exposure for your restaurant, you can cater the food for the tournament or you can host the awards reception at your restaurant. In return for your "sponsorship" you should have your restaurants name on all printed material, hang a banner at the golf tournament and if there is any media supporting this event, you should be recognized as a sponsor. For the most media coverage and exposure in the community, you could actually coordinate the entire golf tournament. This takes some planning, dedication, and is time consuming, but it is a great way to work with and help a charity (which can be one you start.) This type of tournament can develop into an annual tradition.

Walk-a-thons are a simple type of charity sponsorship. By supplying drinks or refreshments for the walkers, you can have your restaurant on all printed material, including the shirts that are typically given to all participants and gain media exposure as a sponsor. Unless of course, you and your employees may want to actually walk and participate in raising money for the charity. This would also serve as great exposure for the restaurant.

Charitable Luncheons & Dinners are yet another way to partner with a charity. You can handle these in a multitude of ways. You can sponsor a luncheon or diner by providing your facility for the function and donate the food and beverages or you may elect to cater at a remote location. If donating the food and beverage is not in your budget, you can ask the charity to cover your costs for food, beverage and labor. In this case, they may sell tickets for $25.00 per person, your costs are $10.00 per person, and the charity still makes $15.00 per person. In this situation, you should not attempt to make a profit on the event. Your profit will come from the exposure and the reputation you gain from hosting such charitable events.

Affinity Partnerships-can be formed with nonprofit organizations with the help of your suppliers in a number of ways. For example, you could donate $.25 to your charity for every Coke product sold. This not only benefits your restaurant; it allows Coke to gain exposure in the community as well. In return, you can ask Coke to donate product which can offset the $.25 donation you make.

Taste-of-the-Town-is a fundraising event that features many of the community restaurants. The event coordinator will sell tickets to members of the community and ask the participating restaurants to donate samplings of their food. The participating restaurants will set up a display table with their samplings. The marketing exposure for an event like this is well worth the expense of the donations. This type of event will get media coverage before, during and after the event. Your restaurant will be included in all printed material. Hint: you should work with the coordinator and find the "best location" to set up your display table.

Educational Tie-In's—These would be events related to the schools system. Some ideas are sponsoring teacher of the month, student of the month, most improved student, straight A students and perfect attendance. You can achieve sponsorship by providing gift certificates, appetizer cards or dessert cards. Sponsorships such as "Project Graduation" may require the donation of food and beverage for an alcohol free party. The opportunities are limitless. There are so many clubs and organizations within the school system that are always in need of assistance. You might even consider giving student tours of your restaurant. It can be informative and educational while providing the children a day away from school!

SUMMARY POINTS

- Goodwill cannot be destroyed or taken away
- Involvement with charities will broaden your customer base.
- Limit the amount of "gift certificates as donations" to <u>your</u> meet your budget!
- Involvement in charities can be done in a variety of ways.
- The educational system has many opportunities for sponsorship

CHAPTER 7

"GIFT CERTIFICATES"

> "The manner of giving is worth more than the gift"
> -Pierre Cornielle

Gift certificates have become such big business that all owners and managers should understand the importance of gift certificate sales. The reason gift certificates have become so popular is due to the hectic and rushed lifestyles that have become the norm in almost every household across the country as well as the time it takes to decide what to get someone. Incidentally, what do you get the person who supposedly has everything? A gift certificate to his or her favorite restaurant, or your favorite restaurant. It is simple, it is easy and it is a gift that will be used! No more ugly ties.

How does gift certificate sales benefit you? First it allows others to market your business. It is free publicity. Gift certificates either introduce a new customer to your restaurant or stimulate frequency among existing customers. This leads to increased sales. Second, when a gift certificate is purchased, it is the same as accepting an interest free, tax deferred loan. At the sale, the customer is giving you the money in exchange for the gift certificate. When the gift certificate is redeemed at your restaurant is when you actually "pay back" the loan. Which is also when taxes are realized. In fact there was a restaurant franchise in the Boston area with three restaurants that was able to finance a fourth restaurant on holiday gift certificate sales!

There is also the issue of gift certificate redemption. Estimates nation-wide state that approximately 20% of gift certificates are never redeemed. Although this defeats the original intent of the sale, you still received the money. I consult with a restaurant in Wilmington, DE that sold over $40K in holiday gift certificates. The owner, (also a pool shark) was aware of the redemption percentages and decided to buy a new motorcycle with the estimated 20% of gift certificates that would never be redeemed!

There are three types of people who purchase and give gift certificates to your restaurant. The first group of people is advocates of your restaurant. This group enjoys your restaurant so much that they are willing to personally introduce the recipients, to your restaurant, by way of the gift certificate. This is free promotional activity. These are the greatest customers you can have. The second group are those who know someone who is an advocate of your restaurant, and giving a gift certificate is the type of gift that will denote both value and thought. You should qualify these individuals when they come into your restaurant. They have made the decision to come to your restaurant and purchase a gift certificate. This is an opportunity for you to "sell" your restaurant to them and invite them to come back and dine.

The third group are the procrastinators (or drunks who sat at the bar all day) and have waited until the last minute to purchase something very quickly! They purchase the gift certificate out of shear convenience! Keep the drinks flowing!

Periodically, you should remind your customers that you have gift certificates available for sale. "Soft selling" gift certificates through table tent inserts, a note on your menu or an in store display are possible promotional activities you can use to stimulate sales.

During the holiday season I highly recommend taking a more serious approach to selling gift certificates. In fact, you should develop a plan that details a step-by-step process. An example for a Christmas Holiday season promotion could be:

October 1	Communicate to staff the "Holiday" gift certificate contest you plan to conduct for the months of November & December.
October 1	Gift Certificate table tent insert
October 7	Direct mailing to Chamber of Commerce members
October 14	Check presenter inserts
October 21	In store displays (posters)
October 28	An outside banner
November 1	Host an employee meeting to review the gift certificate contest for your staff & motivate the selling!
November 7	Direct mailing to your customer base
November 14	An insert in the Chamber Newsletter
November 21	Review staffing to accommodate the efficiency of the sales process
November 28	Follow up postcards (direct mail) to Chamber Members
December 1	Post contest results for the first month to stimulate interest
December 7	Set daily goals for the staff with daily prizes for reaching the goals.
December 14	Post contest results to stimulate interest and sales activities.
December 21	Continue to post contest results

December 31   End contest. Finalize results. Prepare to see an
                     increase in sales beginning on the 26th and into
                     the first two months of the New Year.

The Christmas holiday is noted for gift giving. By focusing your promotional efforts during the months proceeding the holiday, you can expect a boost in sales for the first quarter. Due to the volume of gift certificate sales, and when the majority of gift certificates are redeemed, many companies reduce or eliminate marketing expenditures in the first two months of the new year.

As I mentioned in the chapter on charity, you will be bombarded with calls for donations from every type of organization, club, charity and association. I do not recommend giving a monetary donation...ever. Your goal in giving a donation is to promote goodwill and to get more people in your restaurant. Giving money will promote goodwill but may never accomplish the goal of getting customers in your restaurant. You should budget the amount of gift certificates you want to donate each month and attempt not to exceed that amount. Get comfortable saying no!

Gift certificates are a benefit you are providing for your customers and for yourself. I will caution that you must properly manage gift certificates. They should be treated just like cash. With the advancements in technology, scanners and printers, counterfeit gift certificates should be a concern. Many companies have elected to use gift cards that can be loaded magnetically. They are easier to handle and much harder to duplicate or counterfeit. The negative associated with the use of gift cards is cost!

SUMMARY POINTS

- Gift certificates sales are a multi-million dollar business
  - They provide a convenience for your customers
    - Gift certificate sales induce trial
  - Gift certificates are an interest free tax deferred loan
- Holiday gift certificate sales stimulate first quarter sales
  - Gift certificates must be properly managed

Case Study

As a franchise consultant for The Melting Pot, I recommended that they implement a Holiday Gift Certificate Program similar to the guideline in this chapter. With the assistance of Todd Dziubek, Vice President of Restaurant Operations, we outlined the program and presented it to the franchise licensees at their Annual Franchise Meeting in October. A bit skeptical at first, the program turned out to be a win-win situation for the franchiser and the franchisees!

The contest generated an increase in gift certificate sales by 51%. Overall sales in the first two months of 2002 have increased by 15%.

The Contest

At the time of the contest, there were 53 Melting Pot restaurants with sales volumes ranging from $600K per year to $3.5M per year. So to make it fair, we divided the stores into three categories based on sales volume. In each category, we awarded two prizes. One for the highest overall sales and one for the largest percentage increase. The prize for the highest sales per store received a percentage of their overall gift certificate sales and $500 for an employee recognition party. The prize for winning the highest percentage increase in each category won $500 for an employee recognition party.

The Conclusion

Six restaurants won a prize. Franchisees were excited that the franchiser contributed the prizes. Gift certificate sales increased from $678,000 to $1,024,000. Gross Sales for the restaurants nationwide over the first two months of 2002 have increased by 15%. The total prize giveaway was $10,000. The increase in sales generated an extra $100,000 in revenue for the first two months of 2002, (based on a 4.5% franchise fee.)

CHAPTER 8

Sports Sponsorships

> Sports are positively essential. It is healthy to engage in sports, they are beautiful and liberal, liberal in the sense that nothing serves quite as well to integrate social classes, etc.
>
> —Anton Pavlovich Chekhov

Youth Team Sponsorship

I recommend sponsoring youth sports teams in your community. The cost varies but it is about $250.00 for the season. With this sponsorship fee, you can usually count on having your name on the shirts, and possibly a banner in the field. By sponsoring youth sports teams, you accomplish two marketing concepts. You are sponsoring a sporting event, which creates goodwill among the families that attend practices and games. Second, you are creating lifelong customers with the "kids". Sponsorship fees are one way to support local youth teams, another opportunity is to host the end of the season party for the team. You could elect to donate the food for the team, but charge for the family and friends that decide to join them. If a picture is worth a thousand words, what is the taste of good food worth?

Sponsoring youth soccer teams is also a great marketing avenue to approach. "Soccer moms" are known to busy with little time to spend cooking dinner. As a sponsor of the team, you can bet these soccer moms will be ordering food "to-go" from your restaurant.

High School Sports

Forget getting your name on the jerseys, it will not happen. The available marketing would be signage in a stadium, a ballpark or gymnasium and program guides for the sport being sponsored. You could trade-out the cost of this by sponsoring a banquette at the end of the season for the athletes, or providing a pre-game meal. The opportunity to partner with private schools is easier. These schools do not have the same funding as public schools do. Therefore they look for ways to reduce costs for awards banquettes and season ending celebrations.

Schools will not be the ones who contact you. You have to contact the schools in your community that you plan to work with. The main contact in a school system for this type of marketing would be the athletic director. The reason you should work directly with the athletic director is so you will not have to deal with each individual coach. Ultimately, the coaches have to get the approval of the athletic director anyway.

College and University Sports

Similar to the high school sponsorships, if there is a college or university in your community, contact the athletic director to discuss marketing opportunities. First, know what marketing you want, and what you are willing to give in return. For example, I provided a pre-game meal for a college basketball team and in return I was given a complimentary ad in the basketball program that was distributed at every home game. In addition, the basketball coach gave the restaurant four season tickets (which I was able to use as incentives for my staff.) Providing pre-game meals can encompass all seasons of the year with the sponsorship of football, baseball, basketball, women's softball etc.

There are options other than pre-game meals and program ads. For instance, during half time of basketball games, a ticket holder is selected to shoot a free throw. There is usually a prize given if the free throw is made. The prize could consist of a dinner for two from your restaurant. The announcer would inform the audience that your restaurant sponsored the half time activities.

Raffles according to ticket numbers during baseball games are a great way to market your restaurant. For example: just after the seventh inning stretch the announcer could say " whoever has ticket number @#$@!% wins a dinner for two to your restaurant!"

If your restaurant is located near a college campus, you may want to explore sponsorship of intramural teams and leagues as well. Grassroots-marketing opportunities exist for this very popular division of the college-sporting world.

Adult League Sports

I favor sponsoring adult team sports (such as softball, volleyball or flag football) if they represent your target market. Sponsoring an adult sport team allows you to network within this segment of the community. Once again, you have to be involved. You must do more than silk screen your restaurant's name on the jersey. You must make sure the team upholds the image you want your restaurant to portray. Next, you want to personally get to know all the players, the friends and family members they bring to the games, the referees and the opposing team's players. By getting involved, these individuals will choose your restaurant when making a dining decision. The reason is because of the need to belong and to be recognized. They will come to your restaurant to see you!

There are many grassroots-marketing opportunities that exist or that can created in relation to sports. You have to know your community. Naturally there will be sports that are indicative to your climate. However, the same basic strategies should still apply.

Professional Sports

Sponsoring professional sports can be expensive. However, there are ways to market your restaurant, which are cost effective. During spring training in Florida, there are many opportunities to partner with the teams. You can sponsor a tailgate cook-out before the game, sponsor the game by giving away an appetizer or dessert for the first 300 fans, give away dinners to randomly selected ticket holders. For minor league sponsorships, you have the opportunity for signage in the outfield.

During professional hockey games, there are opportunities to sponsor "shoot-outs" between periods. At professional basketball games there are opportunities for half-time shoot-outs. The fact is that your grassroots marketing efforts must be congruent with your restaurant.

Summary Points

- Sponsor youth teams for community goodwill and to create lifelong customers
- Explore the possibilities of sponsoring team sports including high school, college, adult leagues & professional.
- The individuals you sponsor are not only potential customers, the are potential employees as well.

CHAPTER 9

Technology

> The knowledge of individual customer needs that companies can capture through technology harkens back to the days when the butcher, baker, and candlestick maker knew their clientele personally.
> -Regis Mckenna

We are in the information age. The acquisition of information, the transfer of information, the assimilation of information and the disbursement of information; these are an asset of every restaurant company competing in today's society. The restaurants that fail to realize this will wake up in a few years and find out it is too late. The competition will have captured the market.

As restaurant owners and managers it is important to understand the advancements in technology and how they relate to the marketing function. Technology has found its place in every industry, no matter how unsophisticated. The restaurant industry, which has been one of the last to embrace technology, is now faced with many options. Industry leaders have advanced reservation systems, inventory management systems, ordering systems, POS systems and interactive training systems, which all assist in building sales and profits.

Database creation and management are the technological advancements that relate to the grassroots marketing function. This concept is not new. It just has a "term" defining it. Most small operators have an advantage over the bigger restaurant chains. Smaller operators have the ability to meet all the customers and get to know them personally. These owners and operators even get to know birthday's of customers, anniversaries and special engagements. That is the advantage smaller operators have over the large, impersonal, chain restaurants.

> "One of the unique things we small companies have over the big guys is the ability to establish personal relationships. Big companies really can't do that. You read about effective organizations, learning organizations, lean and mean organizations, but small companies can be virtuous organizations. It is really hard to think of a huge company being called virtuous. We as small companies can have virtue because we as small companies are basically the embodiment of one or two people, and people can have virtue, while organizations really can't.
> Jim Koch Founder of Boston Beer Company, maker of Sam Adams

Technology has identified the need for large restaurants to operate on the smaller level. Thus, database management companies have developed proprietary software that allows them to manage extremely large amounts of information related to your customers. They accomplish this on an outsourcing basis. Much like you outsource a linen company or cleaning company. These companies will assist in creating a database of your customers either through a simple questionnaire or through electronic credit card processing, (with the consent of your customers.) Once the database is created, the company will then manage the database for you. They do this by sending greeting cards to your customers for their birthdays, holidays and any special occasions. They can send direct mailings informing your customers of menu changes, wine tastings, and special offerings. They will manage your customers however you instruct them to.

Other types of technology related to database creation and management are derived through "online" reservation systems. OpenTable.com is the industry leader in online reservation and database creation via the Internet. Essentially, Opentable.com provides the client with a computer terminal and DSL access. The customers can make reservations online or the traditional way of calling in. If they make the reservation online, the restaurant captures the email address. If the customer calls, the reservationist asks for an email address to send a confirmation of the reservation. Throughout the course of the year, a database will be created of your customers. Opentable.com allows you the flexibility to categorize your customers. You can then send emails to them in relation to the category. For instance, customers who have an interest in wine can be emailed if you host a wine tasting or add a new wine to your menu. Customers interested in fresh seafood can be notified of the daily fresh catch. The system also allows you to create lists of birthdays, anniversaries, and special occasions. You can send emails for different holidays. This type of marketing in known as **just-in-time marketing**. Reminding your customers to make reservations or to dine at your restaurant just prior to the event. The options to manage your database of customers are limitless with this technology.

ISeats.com is another online reservation portal. If you choose to become a client of this company, they allow your customers to make reservations either through your Web site, through iSeatz.com's Web site or through partners such as Travelocity.com or Citysearch.com. Then iSeatz contacts the restaurant either by fax or phone. Iseatz.com is in the process of integrating with the Aloha (Point Of Sale) system. For the restaurants with the Aloha system, reservations will be confirmed via the Internet.

These are just a few of the technological advancements that are related to the grassroots marketing function. Database management is important regardless of technology. For "mom and pop" restaurants, database management is just a fancy term for knowing your customers and being able to add a personal touch. However, technology will allow for larger, impersonal, chain restaurants to achieve a more personalized approach to customer service. This personalizes approach will lead to increased sales and stimulate loyal patronage.

SUMMARY POINTS

- It is important to understand the technology as it relates to the restaurant industry.
- Database management is closely related to the grassroots marketing function.
- Database management has the potential to allow large, impersonal, restaurants to become more personalized which leads to increased sales.

CHAPTER 10

Direct Mail

> A little knowledge about direct mail can definitely be dangerous!
> -Richard F. Gershon, Ph. D.

I left direct mailing as the last grassroots marketing tactic. Direct mail should be used as integral part of the marketing plan. It can be target specific, it can be time sensitive, it is easily measurable and it is cost effective. Statistically, direct mail responses are only 1% to 2%. However, these percentages can be improved with a follow up phone calls. Even if these mailings fail to generate immediate results, it creates a top of the mind awareness.

I mentioned in earlier chapters that direct mail can be used in conjunction with each of the other tactics, or as an extension of your involvement. As a member of the Chamber of Commerce, you have access to mailing lists of all members. This list is typically a comprehensive list of businesses in your community, however, it can be segmented by the size of the company based on number of employees or sales by number of employees or sales. If you work closely with a charity, (as I recommend you do) there are opportunities to use their list of supporters for your direct mail efforts.

Some charities have lists with over 5000 supporters in many communities. This is based on the strength of the charity and the size of the community. Partnering with a charity for Grand Openings is a great way to utilize their lists. You can donate a portion of the "Grand Opening" sales in exchange for the charity sending out invitations to all supporters in their database. That is correct. They will send the mailings!

As a sponsor of sports teams, either through the educational system, the city, or county government, or a sports organization, lists of their participants, their families and other sponsors may be available if you request. And let's not forget about technology. If you build a database of your customers, you will have the ability to send them holiday cards, birthday cards, newsletters, press releases, articles or advertisements about specials. This can be done extremely cost effective if you utilize email addresses.

I definitely recommend using direct mail as an integral part of your holiday gift certificate campaign. If your restaurant sells gift certificates during the holiday season, you can boost your sales with the implementation of an aggressive direct mail campaign. Use your all the lists available to you. Especially those that best mirror your target market.

Direct mail can be used in many ways. Following is a small list that you can add to as you explore the opportunities.

1. Build the mailing list.
2. Boost sales.
3. Inform customers about specials, features or tastings.
4. Use the list to conduct research.
5. Use the list to publicize newsworthy information.
6. Use the list to keep in touch with your customers. Birthdays, holidays etc.
7. Make direct sales for gift certificates or merchandise you may sell.

SUMMARY POINTS

- Direct mail is target specific, cost effective, easily measured
- Direct mail response rates can be improved with follow up
- Direct mail will be very effective if used in addition to the other grassroots marketing efforts.

CHAPTER 11

Conclusion

Emerson said that if you build a better mousetrap the world will beat a path to your door, and that may have been true then…but it's not true now. No one will come. You have to package and promote that mousetrap. Then they will come.

-Charles Gillete

There are literally hundreds of grassroots marketing activities that restaurant owners, managers and staff members can be involved in. All marketing efforts must be reflective of your restaurant, and geared to your target market. Grassroots marketing begins with the physical structure of the restaurant, and the proper management of internal operations. It is at this point that you can focus on external activities. Grassroots marketing can be as simple as wearing a shirt or hat with your restaurant's logo to the local grocery store or as complex as establishing and organizing a fundraising, charity golf tournament.

As the owner or operator, you have the ability to build your customer base. As I addressed earlier, lifelong customers are essential to the growth of your business. You accomplish this by creating personal relationships that satisfy your customer's need to belong.

Regardless if you are a chain restaurant or an independent operating with only one location, you have the opportunity to build a reputation within the community. This requires personal involvement in activities related to your neighborhood. From school partnerships to charity sponsorships, the opportunity to build and maintain the reputation as a community business will solidify your reputation, leading to an increased customer base among the members of your community.

It is imperative that you educate yourself on the technological advancements that are rapidly changing our business environment. It is only then that you will be able to protect your business and maintain your customer base. Technology has the potential to alter our industry, change the rules of competition and create new ways for our competitors to outperform us. However, there is no substitute for quality service, excellent food and personal relationships that are established and nurtured between you, your staff and your customers.

If you have any questions regarding any of these grassroots marketing ideas, other aspects of the marketing function or restaurant operations please contact me.

Reader's Digest, a quote found in "Promoting Issues and Ideas" by M. Booth and Associates, Inc.

"…if the circus is coming to town and you paint a sign saying 'Circus Coming to the Fairground Saturday', that's **advertising**. If you put the sign on the back of an elephant and walk it into town, that's **promotion**. If the elephant walks through the mayor's flowerbed, that's **publicity**. And if you get the mayor to laugh about it, that's **public relations**." If the town's citizens go the circus, you show them the many entertainment booths, explain how much fun they'll have spending money at the booths, answer their questions and ultimately, they spend a lot at the circus, that's **sales**.

Adam Barringer
518 W. Patterson Street
Lakeland, FL 33803

Email: abarri1705@aol.com

APPENDIX I

Appendix I

Basic Marketing Plan

1.)	Goals & Objectives: short term, long term
2.)	Target Market: Age, income, gender
3.)	Target market needs
4.)	Your strengths, weaknesses, opportunities & threats
5.)	Your competitive position and how you will compete
6.)	Marketing & advertising budget
7.)	Promotional strategies
8.)	Action plans
9.)	Plan execution
10.)	Plan evaluation

APPENDIX II

Appendix II

Grassroots Assessment Worksheet

<u>Restaurant facility</u>

Traditional marketing consists of 4 P's. Product, price, promotion and place. "Place" in our industry is the actual restaurant, which is a very important aspect of the entire marketing plan.

What is the condition (appearance) of the exterior of your restaurant?
_____ Great _____ Good _____ Poor
What is the condition (appearance) of the interior of your restaurant?
Dining Room:
_____ Great _____ Good _____ Poor
Restrooms:
_____ Great _____ Good _____ Poor
Kitchen:
_____ Great _____ Good _____ Poor

Is there an opportunity to improve appearance from the customer's, vendor's or employee's perspective?
_____ Yes _____ No

If Yes,
explain:_____

Vendor Relations

Creating good vendor relations is just plain good business sense! Relationship marketing does not have to be with just your customers.

What type of grassroots marketing activities does your restaurant engage in to create great relationships with your vendors?

Does your restaurant have opportunity to establish better relationships with supply chain partners?

_____ Yes _____ No

Explain:_____
_____

Service Staff/Sales Staff

Your service staff is your sales force. 70% of your customers view a "sales-person" as the store. A well-trained employee with a positive attitude knows how to identify our customers needs, expectations and wants. They try to exceed our customer's expectations. This type of employee will have a positive affect on repeat sales. A poorly trained, stressed out employee will have a negative affect on sales. Successful restaurants market themselves in ways that develop rapport, trust, and long-term relationships with their customers

How many people are on your service staff?_____

What are their sales responsibilities? _____
_____

Is your restaurant properly staffed to adequately sell and provide great service to you customers?
_____ Yes _____ No

(If No, how many additional employees do you need to hire?_____)

How is the training of you staff?

_____ Great _____ Good _____ Poor

How often do you conduct ongoing training classes or seminars?

_____ Weekly _____ Monthly _____ Other(specify)
_____

Explain the ongoing training:
_____
_____
_____
_____
_____
_____

Identify the strengths & weaknesses of your service staff.
_____

Owner

As the owner of the restaurant, we discussed how important it is to get to know your customers. An estimated 83% of people will return to a restaurant if they have sincere contact with an owner.

How many of your customers do you know by their first name?_____

Who are they?

_____

_____

_____

_____

How many of your customers do you know by their last name? _____

_____

If different from above, who are they?

_____

_____

_____

Do you have a grassroots marketing opportunity for building relationships with your customers?
Explain:_____

_____

_____

Word-of-mouth

To be successful in the restaurant business, you need to cultivate positive word-of–mouth marketing. It is the most effective way to market your restaurant. The power of word-of-mouth marketing multiplies exponentially, whether good or bad. Customers appreciate restaurant owners who appreciate them.

How do you promote word of mouth advertising?

_____

Complaint Marketing

A dissatisfied customer will tell at least nine other people, who in turn will tell their friends and family as well. Dissatisfied customers can ruin a restaurant's reputation. You must truly believe that complaints are not something to be avoided, but as an opportunity for continual improvement. Negative word-of-mouth can be four to five times more powerful than positive word-of-mouth.

How does your restaurant handle complaints?

_____

Participation in Organizations

Meet, greet and be sweet. The more people you are able to meet and be nice, friendly, courteous and professional to can only enhance the chance that those people will become your customers. Joining organizations and being active gives your more opportunities to market your business.

What groups or professional organizations are you involved in?

_____

Why did you join these organizations?
_____ To support the organization

_____ For networking opportunities
_____ To promote the restaurant
_____ Other (specify)_____
Have you used you membership in these organizations to effectively promote your restaurant?
_____ Yes _____ No
If yes, how?
_____ Served as public spokesperson for the organization
_____ Served on committee as chairman or executive officer
_____ Told other members about the restaurant
_____ Hosted meeting at the restaurant
_____ Catered food or beverages at remote location for meetings
_____ Other (specify)_____

What are other marketing activities you can conduct within these organizations to promote your restaurant?

_____

Charity Involvement

Charity involvement is one of the most effective tactics in which to utilize the promotional function of marketing plan. Sponsoring community events, charities and nonprofit organizations can build goodwill for your restaurant and broaden your customer base. Customers like to do business with companies that give back to the community. Press releases tied to charity functions help to strengthen your image and reputation. Properly executed, you gain exposure before, during, and after the event.

What type of charitable activities has your restaurant participated in?
_____ $$Donations

_____ Luncheon
_____ Dinner
_____ Golf tournament
_____ Walk-a-thon
_____ Gift Certificates
_____ Other(specify)_____

What type of promotional activity did you receive as a result of your charitable involvement?
_____ Listed as a sponsor in all printed material
_____ Recognized at event
_____ Media coverage
_____ Other (specify)_____
_____ Unsure
_____ None

Publicity Efforts

Publicity is free advertising for your restaurant through newspaper articles, radio, and television (news & talk shows.) Public relations is the strategy for presenting your restaurant to the public. Publicity is one of the best marketing tools because it works and it is free!

Has your restaurant sought publicity?

_____ Yes _____ No

Explain:_____

_____

_____

If yes, in what media?

_____

_____

Who initiated the contact with media?

_____ Representative of the restaurant

_____ A representative of the media

Who was the media contact? (Include address & phone #)

_____

_____

_____

Did the publicity efforts result in stories?

_____ Yes _____ No

If yes, what kind of stories were written about your restaurant?

_____

_____

_____

_____

Have you submitted press releases?

_____ Yes _____ No

If yes,
explain:_____

Gift Certificates

As I stated earlier, properly executing a gift certificate sales program will generate sales and profits!

Does your restaurant sell gift certificates?

_____ Yes _____ No

If yes, do you actively promote gift certificate sales?

_____ Yes _____ No
If yes, explain:_____

Sports Sponsorships

Sponsoring sports teams is another aspect of the promotional mix. You have to decide of it fits your restaurant's image. Sports sponsorships can be target specific based on the type of sport, or the geographic location where the sporting activity takes place.

Has your restaurant sponsored any sports teams or sporting events?
_____ Yes _____ No
If Yes, explain:_____

What type of promotions did you receive in return for your sponsorship?
_____ Restaurant name or logo on team uniform
_____ Sinage in gymnasium, arena, stadium or ball park
_____ Name logo in program or printed material
_____ Media coverage
_____ Other (specify)_____

Technology

Technology is part of every day business, in every business. Has your restaurant embraced technology? I hope the answer is YES. If not, you need to! I can tell you from research and experience every major and minor restaurant chain is dialed in, dialed up, hooked up, connected, Interneted, intraneted, uploaded, downloaded and now I am getting over loaded!

How does your restaurant use technology for grassroots marketing?

_____ Database management

_____ Email lists

_____ Newsletters

_____ Web site

      Does your web site allow for online reservations?_____

      Can your customers place orders via the internet?_____

      Does your web site collect customer data? _____

_____ None

Direct Mail

Direct mail should be part of your promotional mix. Direct marketing is targeted-you know exactly who you marketing to; it is measurable-you can track the effectiveness of your efforts.

Have you used direct mail to reach your customers?

_____ Yes _____ No

If yes, what types?

_____ Post cards

_____ Email

_____ Flyers

_____ Letters

_____ Other (specify)_____

What material did you send to these customers?

_____

_____

Where did you get the list of potential customers?

_____

_____

Who designed the direct mail piece?

_____

_____

Who performed the actual tasks associated with the mailing?

_____

_____

How frequently has your restaurant used direct mailings?

_____

_____

Was the direct mail campaign successful?

_____ Yes _____ No

Explain:_____

_____

_____

APPENDIX III

Appendix III

Grassroots Plan & Goal Sheet

So far, we have covered the general concepts of grassroots marketing and hopefully completed the worksheet in appendix 1. You should now have several ideas or areas of opportunity for increasing sales through grassroots marketing efforts.

Developing the Grassroots Marketing Plan and Goal Sheet

What sales goals does the restaurant want to achieve this year?
_____
_____
What are the desired profits based on sales?
_____
_____
Who is our target market?
_____
_____
How many customers must be served in order to hit the projected sales goal?
_____
_____

The Restaurant Facility Action Plan

What opportunities do we have with the physical structure of our restaurant?

_____

_____

What are the actions needed to complete these initiatives?

_____

_____

What are the costs associated with these initiatives?

_____

_____

Who will be responsible?

_____

_____

What is the time frame to start and finish?

_____

_____

_____

Vendor Action Plan

What opportunities do we have with our vendor relations?

What are the actions needed to complete these initiatives?

What are the costs associated with these initiatives?

Who will be responsible?

What is the time frame to start and finish?

Service Staff Action Plan

What opportunities do we have with our service staff?
_____
_____

What are the actions needed to complete these initiatives?
_____
_____
_____

What are the costs associated with these initiatives?
_____
_____
_____

Who will be responsible?
_____
_____
_____

What is the time frame to start and finish?
_____
_____
_____

Owner/Management Action Plan

What opportunities do I have to build sales through grassroots marketing?
_____
_____

What are the actions that I need to complete these initiatives?
_____
_____
_____

What are the costs associated with these initiatives?
_____
_____
_____

What is the time frame to start and finish?
_____
_____
_____

Word-of-Mouth Action Plan

What opportunities do we have to strengthen our word-of-mouth marketing?

_____

_____

What are the actions needed to complete these initiatives?

_____

_____

_____

What are the costs associated with these initiatives?

_____

_____

_____

Who will be responsible?

_____

_____

_____

What is the time frame to start and finish?

_____

_____

_____

Complaint Marketing Action Plan

What opportunities do we have with to improve how we handle complaints?

_____

_____

What are the actions needed to complete these initiatives?

_____

_____

_____

What are the costs associated with these initiatives?

_____

_____

_____

Who will be responsible?

_____

_____

_____

What is the time frame to start and finish?

_____

_____

_____

Community Involvement Action Plan

What opportunities do we have to become more involved in our community?

_____

_____

What are the actions needed to complete these initiatives?

_____

_____

_____

What are the costs associated with these initiatives?

_____

_____

_____

Who will be responsible?

_____

_____

_____

What is the time frame to start and finish?

_____

_____

_____

Charity Action Plan

What opportunities do we have to become more involved in charitable functions or to partner with charities?

_____

_____

What are the actions needed to complete these initiatives?

_____

_____

_____

What are the costs associated with these initiatives?

_____

_____

_____

Who will be responsible?

_____

_____

_____

What is the time frame to start and finish?

_____

_____

_____

_____

Gift Certificate Action Plan

What opportunities do we have to promote the sale of gift certificates?
_____
_____

What are the actions needed to complete these initiatives?
_____
_____
_____

What are the costs associated with these initiatives?
_____
_____
_____

Who will be responsible?
_____
_____
_____

What is the time frame to start and finish?
_____
_____
_____

Sports Sponsorship Action Plan

What opportunities do we have to get more involved with local sports?

What are the actions needed to complete these initiatives?

What are the costs associated with these initiatives?

Who will be responsible?

What is the time frame to start and finish?

Technology Action Plan

What opportunities do we have to utilize technology within our grass-roots marketing plan?

_____

_____

What are the actions needed to complete these initiatives?

_____

_____

_____

What are the costs associated with these initiatives?

_____

_____

_____

Who will be responsible?

_____

_____

_____

What is the time frame to start and finish?

_____

_____

_____

Direct Mail Action Plan

What opportunities do you have to market your restaurant utilizing direct mail?

_____

_____

What are the actions needed to complete these initiatives?

_____

_____

_____

What are the costs associated with these initiatives?

_____

_____

_____

Who will be responsible?

_____

_____

_____

What is the time frame to start and finish?

_____

_____

_____

APPENDIX IV

Appendix IV

Grassroots & Promotional Schedule Example

January	February	March	April	May	June
New Years	Valentines Day	St. Patrick's	April	Mother's Day	Father's Day
		Easter		Memorial .Day	
	Begin	*Begin St.*			*Father's*
	Valentine	*Patrick's Day*	*Spring Break*	*Project*	*Day*
	promo Feb 1	*promo on 10th.*	*Taste of*	*Graduation*	*Giveaway!*
Chamber of	*End Feb 14.*	*Run 1 week.*	*Tampa*		*Begin June 1*
Commerce				*Mother's Day*	
Business		*FRA Meeting*		*Charity Ball to*	
After Hours	*FRA Meeting*	*March 5th*		*sponsor Cystic*	
Jan 15th	*Feb 5th.*			*Fibrosis*	
July	August	September	October	November	December
4th of July	Labor Day	Labor Day	Halloween	Thanksgiving	Christmas
	Review staffing		*Sponsor*	Veteran Day	Promote
Begin	*levels for back*		*American*		holiday
Billboard	*to school*	*Labor day*	*Heart*		office parties
to boost	*Coordinate*	*weekend*	*Association*	**Major focus**	
summer	*newspaper*	*extravaganza*	*Halloween*	**on Gift**	
time sales.	*advertising*		*Fund Raiser*	**Certificate**	Focus on
	with help		**Start**	**program**	selling gift
	wanted		**Holiday Gift**		certificates
			Certificate		
			Contest		

Blank Grassroots & Promotional Schedule

January	February	March	April	May	June
New Years ———— ———— ———— ———— ———— ———— ———— ————	Valentines Day ———— ———— ———— ———— ———— ———— ———— ————	St. Patrick's Day Easter ———— ———— ———— ———— ———— ———— ————	———— ———— ———— ———— ———— ———— ———— ———— ————	Mother's Day Memorial .Day ———— ———— ———— ———— ———— ———— ————	Father's Day ———— ———— ———— ———— ———— ———— ———— ————
July	August	September	October	November	December
4th of July ———— ———— ———— ———— ———— ———— ———— ————	———— ———— ———— ———— ———— ———— ———— ————	Labor Day ———— ———— ———— ———— ———— ———— ————	Halloween ———— ———— ———— ———— ———— ———— ————	Thanksgiving Veteran Day ———— ———— ———— ———— ———— ————	Christmas ———— ———— ———— ———— ———— ———— ————

APPENDIX V

Appendix V

Glossary of Marketing Terms & Definitions

Reference:Evans & Berman, 1997, <u>Marketing</u>,7th Edition,Prentice-Hall

Advertising: Paid, nonpersonal, communication through media, regarding goods, services, organizations, people, places, and ideas that are transmitted through various media by business firms, government and other non-profit organizations, and individuals who are identified in the advertising message as sponsors.

Advertising Agency: An organization that provides a variety of advertising related services to clients. Agencies are often responsible for launching a variety of services-campaigns, account management, media planning, creative tasks of theme, design & copywriting, below the line services, research and other tasks.

Advertising Themes: The overall appeal used in a campaign.

All-You-Can Afford Method: After first allocating the budget to all other marketing expenses, the residual funds are allocated to promotions.

Benchmarking: Setting standards that compare favorable with the best companies in the same industry, innovative companies in other industries, direct competitors or prior actions by the company itself.

Boston Consulting Group (BCG): A matrix that classifies each strategic business unit in relation to market share and annual industry growth. The matrix has four cells–star, cash cows, question mark and dogs.

Brand: A name, term, design, symbol or any feature that distinctively identifies a particular good or service.

Brand Equity: A financial value attributed to brand name that is above and beyond the level justified by product quality.

Brand Extension: Applying an established brand name to a new product/s.

Brand Image: Perception people hold about a brand.

Brand Loyalty: Consistent repurchase of and preference for the same brand reducing time, thought and risk.

Brand Mark: A symbol, design, or distinctive coloring or lettering that cannot be spoken.

Brand Name: A word, letter, number, group of words or phrase that can be spoken.

Broad Price Policy: Incorporating short term and long term pricing goals that sets the overall direction of the firm's pricing efforts and makes sure that it is consistent with the marketing mix, target market and image.

Bundled Price: Basic product + options + customer service for one total price.

Business Analysis: Detailed review, projection, analysis of demand, costs, break-even points, competition, capital investments and profitability for new firms or products.

Cause-Related Marketing: A special promotion whereby profit oriented firms allocated a portion of the purchase price for a non-profit cause.

Cease-and-Desist Order: A legal order that requires a firm to stop a particular promotion that is deemed misleading and modify a message accordingly for consumer protection.

Chain-Ratio Method: Sales forecasting which starts with general market information and then computes a series of more specific information that finally yields a sales forecast.

Channel Length: Levels of independent members along a distribution channel.

Channel Members: Organizations or people participating in the distribution process–manufacturers, wholesalers, retailers, service providers, and consumers.

Channel of Communication / Communication Process:–mechanism whereby the source develops a message, transmits the message via a medium to an audience and receives feedback from the audience.

Channel of Distribution: All the organizations or people involved in the distribution process.

Channel Width: Number of independent members at any one stage or level of distribution–e.g. number of retailers of a product.

Class-Action suit: A legal action on behalf of many affected consumers.

Clutter: The number of ads found in a single program (TV/Radio) or issue (magazines/newspapers) of a medium.

Co-Branding: Using two or more brand names with the same product to benefit of the branding benefits of each.

Cognitive Dissonance: When a consumer experiences doubts about the wisdom of a particular purchase.

Comparative Messages: Implicitly or explicitly comparing goods/services with other firm's offerings.

Competition Based Pricing: Prices set according to competitor's prices rather than on demand/supply or cost—these prices could be above, below or at par with competition.

Competitive Parity Method: Allocating budget based on competitor's actions. Concentrated Marketing: Targeting one well-defined market with one specific marketing strategy.

Concept Testing: Stage in the new product planning process where a few consumers are 'exposed' to the product to measure their attitudes and intentions towards the product.

Consumer demographics: Quantifiable characteristics of the population—they are easy to identify, collect, measure and analyze.

Consumerism: Activities that are designed to protect people from practices that violate their rights as consumers.

Consumer Price Index: Monitoring tool of the cost of living, measuring monthly and yearly inflation.

Consumer Products: Those that are designed for the final consumer for personal or household use.

Convenience Products: Those bought with a minimum of effort as consumer has knowledge of product attributes prior to shopping or has an emergency.

Cooperative Advertising: Two or more firms sharing advertising costs

Corporate Culture: Organization-wide shared values, norms, and practices communicated to and followed by all its employees.

Customer Satisfaction: The match between customer's expectations and actual performance of a good/service including customer service.

Customer Service: Those identifiable but intangible activities undertaken by a seller in conjunction with the basic goods/services it offers.

Database Marketing: To identify and alert those customers and prospects from a database that fall in the category of the best possible purchasers for a given offer at a given point of time.

Demand Patterns: Indicates the uniformity of diversity of consumer demand for particular categories of goods/services.

Derived Demand: Organizational consumers demand for goods/services is based on the anticipated demand by their customers for specific g/s.

Differential Advantages: unique features that cause consumers to patronize one particular firm and not the other.

Differentiated Marketing/Multiple Segmentation: Targeting two or more well-defined market segments with distinct and tailor-made marketing strategies for each.

Diffused Demand: A demand pattern in which consumer demand are diverse and no clear clusters are identifiable.

Direct Marketing: Marketing or advertising that call for immediate action through mail, phone, PC.

Direct Selling: Selling through personal contacts with the customer.

Diversification: Firm becomes involved with new g/s aimed at new markets.

Dog: A quadrant in BCG that depicts an SBU with low market share in a low growth industry. A dog has cost disadvantages and low growth opportunities.

Dumping: Selling a product in foreign countries at a price much lower than those prevailing in domestic market or below the cost of production or both.

80-20 Principle: A large proportion of profit or sales comes from a small proportion of customers, products or territories.

Electronic Data Interchange: Allows firms to exchange data via computer linkups.

Ethical Behavior: Honest and proper conduct

Global Marketing: Advanced form of international marketing addressing global customers, markets and competition.

Global Marketing Approach: International Marketing strategy that combines global and local approaches—standardized and non-standardized features with home-office control and still be sensitive and responsive to local needs.

Goods/Services Continuum: Categorizes products along a scale from pure goods to pure services.

Green Marketing: Socioecological marketing that takes into account environmental ramifications for the whole society.

Growth Stage in PLC: Sales increase rapidly and a few more firms enter the industry and the market has substantial potential.

Household: A person or group of persons, related or unrelated, occupying a housing unit.

Independent Media: Communication vehicles not controlled by a firm, yet influence government, consumer and public perceptions of that firm's products and overall image.

Individual (Multiple) Branding: Separate brands used for different items or product lines sold by a firm.

Industrialized of Services: Improves service efficiency and product variability by using hard, soft and hybrid technologies.

Industrial Marketing: Business to Business marketing B2B

Industrial Products: G/S purchased for use in the production of other g/s, operation of a business or resale to other consumers.

Institutionalized Advertising: Used when the advertising goal is only to enhance company image.

Integrated Marketing Communications (IMC): A comprehensive plan that integrates a variety of communication–advertising, PR, personal selling, sales promotion to provide the maximum consistency, impact, and clarity.

International Marketing: Involves marketing g/s outside a firm's domestic country.

Introduction Stage of the PLC: The period during which only one or two firms have entered the market and competition is limited.

Joint Venture/Strategic Alliance: When a firm agrees to combine some aspects of its manufacturing and/or marketing efforts with those of a foreign company so as to share expertise, costs and influence.

Jury of Executive or Expert Opinion: A method of sales forecasting by which the management of a firm or experts meet, discuss and set sales estimates.

Just JIT Inventory System: Reducing inventory and ordering more often and in lower quantity, depending on customer demand.

Just JIT Marketing: Creating customer demand by recognizing important dates such as birthdays and holidays.

Market Development: Firm seeks greater sales of present products from new markets or new product uses.

Marketing: The anticipation, management and satisfaction of demand through the exchange process.

Marketing Mix: Integrating four Ps—Product, Place (distribution), Promotion (advertising, PR, sales promotion), Price.

Marketing Myopia: A shortsighted, narrow-minded view f marketing and its environment.

Marketing Research: Systematically gathering, recording and analyzing information about specific issues related the marketing of g/s, organizations, people, places and ideas.

Marketing Strategy: The detailed planning and analysis, which includes using the marketing mix to fulfill organizational goals.

Market Penetration: Increasing sales of present g/s in its present markets through more intensive distribution & promotion and competitive pricing.

Market Segmentation: Subdividing a market into clear subsets of customers that have the same needs, attitudes or act in the same way.

Massed Promotion: Efforts concentrated in peak periods like holidays.

Maturity Stage PLC: The market is saturated, sales stabilize, many firms enter to capitalize on the still sizable demand.

Me Generation: Lifestyle that emphasizes self-fulfillment, self-expression and being good to oneself.

Microenviroment: Those factors that have a direct impact on firm—distribution intermediaries, competitors, consumers and internal factors within organization.

Missionary Salesperson: Sales support person who gives out information on g/s, describes attributes, answers questions and hands out brochures and literature.

Monopolistic Competition: Several firms in an industry, each offering a unique marketing mix based on price or non-price factors.

Multinational Firm: Corporate HQ based in the domestic market but which accounts for less than 50% of sales and profits.

Objective-and-Task Method: Promotional budget in which a firm sets promotion goals, determines activities to satisfy them and then establishes the proper budget.

Odd Pricing: Selling price below even/round dollar values e.g. US$9.99.

Oligopoly: A few large firms account for most industry sales.

Opinion Leaders: To those whom consumers turn to for advice and information via face-to-face communication.

Perceived Risk: The uncertainty a consumer believes exists as a outcome of a purchase, which may be right or wrong, and is divided into functional, physical, financial, social, psychological, and time.

Personality: The sum total of an individual's enduring internal psychological traits that make the person unique.

Personal Selling: Through oral, generally face-to-face communication with prospective buyers.

Porter Generic Strategy Model: Two key marketing planning concepts: Competitive scope (broad or narrow target) and competitive advantage (lower cost or differentiation)

Post-Purchase Behavior: When further purchases and/or revaluation of the product are undertaken.

Predatory Pricing: Illegal practice of large firms cutting price below costs in select places to eliminate small and local competitors.

Prestige Pricing: Consumers will not buy g/s at prices considered low.

Price: Value of a g/s for seller and buyer.

Price Ceiling: The maximum amount consumers will pay for a g/s.

Price Discrimination: Setting two or more distinct prices for a product, to appeal to different consumers.

Price Elasticity of Demand: Buyer sensitivity to changes in price and the quantities they will purchase.

Price-Floor Pricing: Determining the lowest price at which it is worthwhile to increase the amount of g/s it makes available for sale.

Price-Guarantees: Assure resellers that the prices they pay are the lowest available.

Price Leadership: One or a few firms are the first to announce price changes and others follow suit.

Price Lining: Selling products at a range of prices with each representing a distinct level of quality.

Price-Quality Association: Concept that high prices represent high quality and low prices represent low quality.

Price Wars: Firm continually undercutting each other's prices to attract consumers.

Primary Data: Information gathered to address a specific issue or problem.

Private Brands: Use names designated by resellers–wholesalers or retailers.

Product: An idea, a tangible entity, or service or any combination that consists of a bundle of attributes capable of exchange or use.

Product Development: Developing new or modified products to appeal to present markets.

Product Differentiation: Consumer perception where a product differs from its competition on any tangible or intangible feature including price.

Product Life Cycle: Introduction, growth, maturity and decline stages of a product and describes sales, competitors, profits, customers and marketing efforts.

Product Line: Group of closely related product items.

Product/Brand Manager System: A level of middle managers, each of whom is responsible for the planning, coordinating and monitoring of the performance of one single or a small group of products/brands. They handle both new and existing products and are involved with all the marketing activities related to their product/s.

Product/Marketing Opportunity Matrix: Market Penetration, Market Development, Product Development and diversification are the four alternative marketing strategies to maintain and/or increase sales.

Product Mix: All the product lines a firm offers–described as width, depth and consistency.

Product Positioning: Map each product in terms of consumer perceptions and desires, competition, other company products and environmental changes.

Product Screening: Stage in new product planning, where poor, unsuitable ideas are weeded out.

Promotion: Any communication used to inform, persuade, and/or remind people about a firm's g/s, image, ideas, community involvement, or impact on society.

Promotion Mix: Overall and specific communication program–advertising, PR, personal selling and/or sales promotion.

Publicity: Form or PR that entail nonpersonal communication that is not paid for by an identified sponsor.

Publicity Types: News publicity, business feature article, service feature articles, finance, product, pictorial, and video news releases, editorial material and emergency publicity.

Public Relations (PR): Any communication to foster a favorable image for g/s, firms, people, places and ideas among various publics–consumers, investors, government, employees etc.

Pure Competition: Products are undifferentiated and competition is intense.

Reach: Refers to the number of people in a medium's audience. The total number of people who are exposed to an ad.

Real Income: The total income earned in a year, adjusted by the rate of inflation.

Rebates: Cash refunds directly from the manufacturer to consumer to increase demand.

Reference Group: The group of people who influence a person's thoughts and actions.

Relationship Marketing: Marketing with the conscious intention of developing and managing long-terms, trusting relationships with customers.

Relative Product Failure: Making a profit but not reaching the profit goals and adversely affecting a firm's image.

Retail Chain: Ownership of multiple outlets.

Retailers: Buy or handle g/s for sale/resale to final consumers.

Retail Franchising: Contractual agreement between a franchiser and a retail franchisee, allowing the latter to run a business under the former's established name and according to contractual clauses and rules.

Retail Store Strategy Mix: Integration of hours, location, assortment, service, advertising, prices, and other factors.

Routine Consumer Decision Making: Buying out of habit and skips steps in the decision making process.

Sales Sales involves most or many of the following activities, including cultivating prospective buyers (or leads) in a market segment; conveying the features, advantages and benefits of a product or service to the lead; and closing the sale (or coming to agreement on pricing and services).

Sales Analysis: Detailed study of sales data to appraise effectiveness of marketing strategy.

Sales Exception Report: Highlights situations where sales goals are not met.

Sales Forecast: Outlines expected sales for a g/s in a specific market and time period.

Sales Management: The planning, implementation and control of sales team covering selection, training, territory allocation, compensation and supervision.

Sales Penetration: The degree to which a firm is meeting its sales potential.

Sales Presentation: Verbal description of a company, specific g/s, its features, benefits, price, service and warranty and a demo.

Sales Promotion: Intended to stimulate consumer purchases and dealer effectiveness through trade shows, premiums, incentives, give-aways, demos, and other routines.

Sales Territory: Consists of the geographic area, customers, and product lines assigned to a salesperson.

SBU Strategic Business Unit: A self-contained division, product line, or product department in an organization with specific market and a head with complete responsibility.

Scrambled Merchandising: When retailers add unrelated g/s.

Selective Demand: For a particular brand.

Selling Against the Brand: When distributors stock famous brands and place high prices on them and sell other brands for lower prices.

Selling Process: Getting leads, contacting customers, ascertaining customer wants, providing sales presentations, Q&A, negotiations and deal closing.

Service Blueprint: Map or flowchart detailing a firm's service process.

Service Gap: Difference between customer expectations and actual service received.

Service Marketing Includes rental, servicing of goods.

Social Marketing: Use of marketing to increase the acceptability of social ideas.

Specialty Products: Particular brands, stores and persons to which consumers are loyal and willing to pay above-average prices.

Speciality Store: A retailer that concentrates on one product line.

Star: A quadrant in BCG that describes a leading SBU with high market share in a high growth industry.

Straight Commission Plan: Salesman's compensation based on sales, profits, customer satisfaction or some other performance indicator.

Straight Extension: International product planning strategy in which the same products are sold in foreign markets.

Straight Salary Plan: Salesperson only paid a flat salary.

Strategic Marketing Plan: Outlines marketing actions, justification, allocation of responsibilities, time period and manner of completion.

Subliminal Advertising: Highly controversial promotion where it is claimed that consumers unconsciously decode a message.

Systems Selling: Selling a combination of g/s, which are integrated with one another.

Tactical Plan: Short-term actions undertaken to implement a marketing strategy

Target Market: A particular group of customers whose needs it proposes to satisfy.

Target Market Strategy: Analyze consumer demand, targeting the market and develop the strategy.

Telemarketing: Calling up prospective customers to solicit business or to set up an appointment for the salesperson.

Test Marketing: Placing a fully developed product in a selected area to observe its actual performance.

Total Quality: To fully satisfy customers in an effective and efficient manner through customer focus, top management commitment, continuous improvement.

Trademark: Brand name, brand mark, or trade character of combination of these that has legal protection.

Uncontrollable Factors: External elements that cannot be directed and affects an organization's performance–consumers, competition, suppliers, government, economy, technology and independent media.

Undifferentiated Marketing: Targeting the whole market with one basic strategy intended to have mass appeal.

VALS: Values and Lifestyle Program that segments customers in terms of demographics and lifestyle factors.

Value Analysis: Comparison of costs and benefits of alternative materials or components so as to reduce cost/benefit ratio of purchases.

Variable Pricing: Alter prices in response to cost fluctuations or differences in consumer demand.

Venture Team: Small, independent departments consisting of a broad range of specialists is involved with a specific new product's entire development process.

Vertical Price Fixing: Manufacturers or distributors seek to control the final selling prices.

Warehousing: Physical facilities to store, identify and sort goods.

Warranty: assurance to consumers that product meets certain standards.

Wheel of Retailing: How low-end strategies can evolve into high-end strategies (full service, high price) and provide opportunities for new firms.

Wholesalers: Buy or handle products and subsequent resale.

Word-of-mouth communication: People expressing opinions and product related experiences to one another.

Notes

Notes

0-595-22318-4